WORLDWIDE ADVENTURE

SOCIETY

THIS BOOK BELONGS TO:
Lillian Ovay

THE
ADVENTURES OF

Lily Huckleberry

in Mexico

by

Audrey Smit & Jackie Knapp

Also in this series:

The Adventures of Lily Huckleberry in Scandinavia
The Adventures of Lily Huckleberry in Japan

ISBN: 978-1-7326961-3-6

The Adventures of Lily Huckleberry series is available at special quantity discounts for bulk purchase for wholesale, fundraising, and educational needs. For details, write to wholesale@thislittlestreet.com

Story by Audrey Smit & Jackie Knapp.
Words by Jackie & illustrations by Audrey.

Printed in China.

The Adventures of Lily Huckleberry is FSC certified. It is printed on chlorine-free paper made with 30% post-consumer waste. It uses only vegetable and soy-based ink.

MIX
Paper from responsible sources
FSC® C102842
FSC
www.fsc.org

Published by This Little Street ™
www.thislittlestreet.com | IG @thislittlestreet

Follow @lilyhuckleberry on Instagram
www.lilyhuckleberry.com

First Edition
10 9 8 7 6 5 4 3 2 1

HI FRIENDS,
CHECK THE END OF THE BOOK
FOR A LETTER FROM ME!

TO THE WILD
ONES WHO DREAM
OF FLYING...

THIS STORY IS
FOR YOU.

In a village where the flowers grow as big as trees,
lives a girl named Lily Huckleberry.

Lily lives in a yellow house
on a silly little street.

The mayor throws pillow fights, the grandmas
zip line to tea time, and the mice, who have a
flair for drama, put on spectacular
plays for the village.

And every morning, Lily dances to the end of
the street, throws her arms in the air, and yells,

"GOOD MORNING.
BEAUTIFUL WORLD!
I'M READY FOR YOU!"

You should try it, especially
if you are grumpy in
the mornings.

One day, Lily and her friend the rabbit-mouse
were running late, late, late to a very
important rehearsal date.

As Lily rushed to put on her flower costume...

WHOOOSH!

A big orange blob flew
straight onto her nose.

"Ahhh!" Lily yelped.
"Who turned out
the lights?"

"Sorry! I thought you were a flower,"
the butterfly said.

"It's all right. What's your name?" Lily asked.

[mah-ree-PO-sah]

"I'm María Marisol Mariposa Monarca."

"María Marisol Mariposa Monarca? That's a great big name!
I'm just Lily Huckleberry. You look sad, María.
Are you okay?"

"Oh Lily, I'm so lost, lost, lost!" María cried.

"You poor little butterfly! How did you get lost?"

[fah-MEE-lia]

"Every fall when it gets cold, mi familia flies a long way
south to Mexico. But I got separated and now I can't
find the way by myself!" María wept.

Lily patted her.
"Don't worry. We'll find your family. I'll help you!"

"Really?"

Lily smiled. "Follow me, I have an idea!"

Inside her room, Lily showed María a globe.

"It's from the Worldwide Adventure Society, and it's magical. When you say the special words, it sends you on an adventure wherever you wish. Let's find Mexico."

Lily spun the globe. "Found it! Close your eyes and hang on tight, María. Let's say the magic words together. Ready?"

"GOODBYE, COLLY WOBBLES!
GOODBYE, BELLY BOBBLES!
TIME FOR BALLYHOO!
TAKE ME TO A HULLABALOO!"

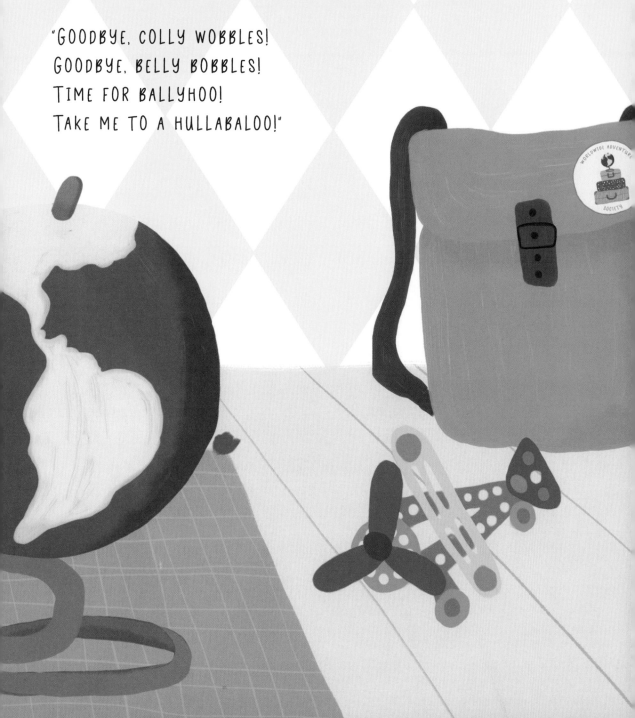

When they opened their eyes, flags of every color filled the sky like confetti.

"Papel picado, my favorite! You did it, Lily Huckleberry. We're in Mexico!" María shouted.

[pah-PEHL pee-KAH-doh]

Happy music filled the air. Lily had a good feeling about this place.

A donkey noticed the girls and put down his trumpet.

"¡Hola! I'm Antonio, the greatest trumpeter in all the land.
What are you chicas doing in my little pueblo?" [poo-EH-blow]

"Can you help us, Antonio? I'm looking for mi familia.
Do you know where the monarchs live?" María asked.

"Oh, you are looking for Mariposa Mountain!
It's a long way from here. Come, I'll show
you a shortcut," he replied.

As they clip-clopped along, Lily noticed the prickly plants. "It's so hot and dusty here, Antonio. Do you like living in the desert?"

"Some people see nothing but heat and dust, but look closer. Do you see the beauty in the open skies and the pink mountains?"

Antonio smiled. "One day I'll find a mariachi band, become famous, and travel the whole wide world. But my heart will always belong to the desert. It's my home."

Lily smiled back. "It's your home sweet home."

"The shortcut is down this ladder through a cave," Antonio pointed. "And there's a great surprise in there! Good luck, chicas."

Lily stared into the black hole.

"It's so dark, my belly is filling with bobbles already. But we're brave, right María?"

María flapped her wings.

"Sí, sí. Adiós, collywobbles!
Let's go, Lily."

BLING! Giant crystals twinkled everywhere!
Lily had seen her share of sparkles, but nothing quite like this.

There were a gazillion crystals and a gazillion ways to go. Can you help Lily and María find the way out?

Thanks! You're a-maze-ing.

SALIDA

At last, they climbed out of the cave and blinked in the bright sun.

"What a razzly-dazzly way to start
an adventure," Lily said.

María looked down the path.

"A village! Someone there has got to know
mi familia. Vámonos, Lily. Let's go!"

[VAH-moh-nos]

As they got closer, the air
buzzed with laughter and music.

Lily looked down the street.

"María! I spy with my little eye...
orange wings fluttering
in the wind. Is that your
family dancing?"

"It looks just like them, Lily!
Let's catch up. Last one
there's a stinky
stink bug!"

But when they got close, Lily yelled,
"Wait! They aren't butter-flies, they are people-flies!"

The people-flies stopped dancing. "What's going on?" María asked.

The grandma people-fly replied, "We're practicing for the
Day of the Dead parade tomorrow in Mexico City. We'll play music
and dance like the mariposas coming home for the winter."

Abuela looked at María. "Why are you flying alone, little mariposa?"

María cried, "I got separated from mi familia, Señora! I can't find them."

[say-NYOH-ra]

[ah-BOO-EH-lah]

"Oh no! Families belong together." Abuela tapped her cane.

"Aha! Come with us to Mexico City. There's a lady there who lives in an enchanted blue house. She's full of magic. She'll know what to do."

WHAT A FUN HULLABALOO!

Everyone talked over each other and sang at the top
of their lungs to the mariachi music.

Abuela opened a suitcase full of...tacos!

"Eat up! I packed two bags full of burritos if you need more.
You can't have a hungry belly on adventures in Mexico!"

The bus dropped the girls off at
a market in Mexico City.

"The blue house is on the other side,"
Abuela pointed. "Good luck!"

"Gracias," María said. "Have fun at the
parade. Flutter like I taught you!"

Lily had never seen so many
colors in one place. She ran through
the stalls, threw her hands
in the air and yelled,

"BEAUTIFUL WORLD,
I'M READY FOR YOU!"

Lily and María found a house
as blue as the sea.

KNOck, kNOck!

A woman with flowers
in her hair opened the door.

"Are you the magic lady?" Lily asked.

The lady laughed.

"¡Hola! I'm Frida. I'm not sure about
magic, but I do have one wild
imagination," she wiggled
her eyebrow and laughed again.

María noticed Frida's beautiful garden.
"Mi familia would love this place! If only
I knew where they were."

"Are you lost? Come inside and tell
me everything," Frida said.

"Churros with your hot chocolate?" Frida asked.

"Yes, please," Lily said. "You have so many paintings in your house, Frida. Did you paint them all?"

"Sí! I love to paint. When I feel lost or sad, I use my imagination to paint my way out."

Lily sighed. "I wish I could paint like you."

"Anyone can be an artist, if you're brave enough to try."

Frida handed Lily a beautiful paintbrush.

"For your adventure. It has special powers to help your ideas come alive."

"How will I know when to use it?" Lily asked.

"Trust me, you'll know," Frida smiled. "Remember, when all seems lost, paint your wings and fly."

Lily beamed at her. "You are magic, I knew it."

Frida wiggled her eyebrow and chuckled.

"As for you, María, I used to go to an island full of butterflies by the canals. Try there?"

Lily and María walked through Mexico City to find the canals.
Everywhere they looked the city was bubbling with life.

"Wow, it's so fun here! Frida didn't say it was going to be one BIG boat party. Mi familia has to be here, they love a good fiesta!"
María giggled.

[fee-ES-tah]

They tried to find a boat to sail to the butterfly island, but all of them were full.

Lily was sad. "Parties aren't much fun when you don't know anyone. I wish we had a friend with a boat."

[ah-MEE-go]

María sighed. "Sí, we need an amigo.
Boy, do we need an amigo."

All of a sudden, a giant sombrero ran right into them.
Under the hat was a boy with twinkling eyes.

"Lily Huckleberry! I'm Felipe. I heard you needed an amigo."
He showed her his Worldwide Adventure Society patch.

"Ah! You're part of the Society?" Lily was thrilled.

Felipe nodded. "Sí! We were born for adventure,
Lily Huckleberry."

"We're trying to get to the butterfly island.
Do you have a boat?" Lily asked.

Felipe winked. "Kind of..."

Lily giggled as she got on the boat.
"This is one handy dandy sombrero, Felipe."

They floated down the canal and sang silly songs.

María smiled. "Adventures are always
better with amigos!"

The three amigos reached the shore and María flew around excitedly.

"So many mariposas, they must be here! Mamá?
Papá? Abuela?" she called.

But these butterflies weren't her butterflies.

"What are we going to do? We're never going
to find them." María's wings drooped and
her eyes filled with big butterfly tears.

Through her tears, María noticed
something in the leaves...

"¡HOLA!"

Out of the flowers burst a goofy lady, spinning
so fast she almost knocked everyone over.

"A luchadora!" Felipe shouted.

[loo-cha-DOH-rah]

"What's a luchadora?" Lily asked.

The lady replied, "Luchadoras are the greatest
wrestlers in all of Mexico. A drumroll for the great
LOCA MARIPOSA. QUEEN OF THE RING.
QUEEN OF THE STING.
QUEEN OF EVERYTHING."

Loca threw her cape
over her shoulder.

"Now, who's crying?
I'm here to save the day."

"Me, me, pick me!" María fluttered.
"Can you help find mi familia?"

Loca pointed to her mask.
"See this? I SPEAK BUTTERFLY.
I BREATHE BUTTERFLY.
I AM BUTTERFLY!
Of course I can help, follow me."

"Looks like you're in good hands.
See you later, alligators!" Felipe waved.

Loca drove the girls to the butterflies, but when they got there, Lily was confused. "Loca, these are piñatas. They aren't alive."

"Son of a tortilla!" Loca poked a butterfly. "Wake up, wake up, wake up!"

Lily shook her head. "These guys can't fly! They're monarchs like María, but they're made of cardboard."

"Oh, you wanted REAL butterflies? Why didn't you say? Come on, I have another idea."

Round and around Mexico they drove,
trying to find María's family. But no matter
where they went, no orange butterflies.

At long last, they reached a sea that looked like bubblegum.
Loca rushed into the water. "Come on chicas,
the butterflies like swimming here."

Lily couldn't believe it. "Loca, you're crazy!
These are flamingos, not butterflies."

"Flamingos? No way! I could have sworn they were butterflies.
They have such colorful wings!" She scratched her head.

Lily slapped her forehead. "Loca Mariposa, do you
know anything about butterflies?"

Loca sat down in the water. "Oh Lily, don't get mad. I'm not telling
butter-lies, I promise. I just get confused sometimes. I know
someone who can help. One last chance?"

Lily and María looked at each other.

"All right. One last chance."

They zipped to the pyramids of the sun and moon. Lily felt small walking along the ancient streets. "It feels so old here. Are these pyramids older than my grandma?"

"Older than anyone's abuela. Some say this is where Mexico started!" Loca said. "My friend Quetzalpapálotl lives here, he'll help you."

[kay-tz-ahl-pah-PAH-lot]

"Ketchup-papaya who?" Lily asked.
María giggled. "Quetzalpapálotl, silly."

"He's at the top," Loca pointed to what looked like a gazillion steps.

"Gracias, Loca! Vámonos, Lily."
María started flying.

Lily gazed up, up, up.
"You're lucky you can fly, María."

CANTINA

On top of the pyramid sat a wild-eyed bird.

Lily walked toward him. "¡Hola! I'm Lily Huckleberry.
Loca said you'd help us find María's family?"

But Quetzal sat and stared at them, not moving, not even blinking.

Lily inched closer. "Excuse me? Can you help?"

"HELP-A-KELP! ZELP-A-WHELP!"
Quetzal hopped around them, muttering.

"This guy doesn't make any sense," María sighed.
"Maybe we should leave."

Just then, Quetzal dipped his wing into a jar and started
painting a rock. He handed it to Lily and said "RIDDLE-DIDDLE."
And with that, he flew away.

"Hey! What's a riddle-diddle?" María yelled after him.

"María, look! The painting is a riddle. First, chase the sunset."
Lily pointed west. "Over there?"

"Sí, sí! What's next? Fly high," María said.

"Fly high?" Lily looked up, but the sky was quiet.

How was Queztal expecting her to fly?

CHASE THE SUNSET

FLY HIGH

NEAR RED MOUNTAIN

FIND YELLOW FLOWERS

"María, I can't fly! Believe me, I've tried, but that gravity thing always wins. Maybe you should go without me."

"No way, José," María said. "Friends don't leave friends on pyramids."

Lily slumped down on the ground and tried to think of something, anything. A pile of dust swooshed into the wind, and for a moment she thought she saw wings.

If only she could make wings out of dust. If only...

All of a sudden, Lily jumped to her feet.

"María! Remember? When all seems lost... paint your wings and fly!"

She opened her backpack...

...grabbed her paintbrush and started painting big swirls in the sky!

Sparkles started SPARKLING.

Glitter started GLITTERING.

The painting started FLUTTERING.

Lily stepped back. "All done."

"You have wings!" María gasped.

Lily fluttered her wings.
"It worked, María. I'm a real people-fly!"

"Sí, sí. You're Lily Mariposa now."

María started flying towards the pink sun.

"Wait!" Lily yelled. "I still don't know how to fly.
What if I fall?"

María circled back.

"You'll never know unless you jump…
I believe in you, Lily!"

Lily stood on the edge.

Her knees were knocking and her belly bobbling.
Could she do it?

Lily gathered every last bit of courage and shouted,

"GOODBYE, COLLY WOBBLES!"

And she jumped…

FLY, LILY, FLY!

"I'm soaring!" Lily loop-de-looped all
over the pretty little sky. She couldn't
even remember being scared.

"Isn't flying fun? Way
better than being a caterpillar,
if you ask me," María floated by the clouds.

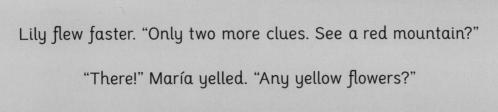

Lily flew faster. "Only two more clues. See a red mountain?"

"There!" María yelled. "Any yellow flowers?"

"Aha!" Lily pointed. "Vámonos, María!"
They flew closer and closer...

...all of a sudden,
thousands of orange
wings fluttered out of the trees.
It was Mariposa Mountain
at last!

A cloud of butterflies surrounded
Lily. "María, your home is better
than all my dreams!"

"I knew you'd love it," María giggled.
"Mamá? Papá? Abuela? Where are you?"

With a frenzy of flapping, María's family swooped over.
"Maria Marisol Mariposa Monarca? Is that you?!" They covered her in
kisses and happy tears. "You're home, you're finally home!"

"This is Lily Huckleberry, she helped me find
my way back," María said.

"Viva Huckleberry!" they cheered.

María's mama kissed Lily's nose.
"My dear Lily, mi casa es tu casa, my home
is your home. Stay as long as you'd like.
Now, let's celebrate!"

[mee kah-sah es too kah-sah]

It was one fabulous fiesta on Mariposa Mountain!

All of their amigos came. They laughed and danced and played music late into the night. Antonio found his band at last, and made plans to travel the whole wide world.

At the end of the fiesta, Felipe gathered everyone together.

"Lily Huckleberry, you were very brave and let your imagination fly to
help a friend. On behalf of the Society, here is your patch to
remember your Mexican hullabaloo," Felipe said.

Lily took her new patch from the butterflies.

"Gracias, amigos. That was one soaring adventure, Mexico!
Now, where should I go next?"

- the End

GULF
OF
MEXICO

PACIFIC
OCEAN

MEXICO
CITY

MEXICAN
Hidden treasures!

CAN YOU FIND COLORFUL ANIMAL FIGURES IN THE MARKET PAGE? THOSE ARE ALEBRIJES, WHIMSICAL CARVINGS REPRESENTING SPIRIT ANIMALS. ACCORDING TO THE ZAPOTEC TRADITION, WHEN BABIES ARE BORN, THEY ARE ASSIGNED A CREATURE TO PROTECT THEM THROUGHOUT THEIR LIVES.

CAN YOU FIND THE MEXICAN FLAG IN THE BOOK? WHAT ANIMALS DO YOU SEE ON IT? THE LEGEND SAYS THAT THE AZTEC PEOPLE, ONE OF THE CIVILIZATIONS OF MEXICO, WOULD KNOW WHERE TO BUILD THEIR CITY ONCE THEY SAW AN EAGLE EATING A SNAKE.

Did you notice a girl in a fancy dress with her parents in Mexico City? She is celebrating her quinceañera, her 15th birthday – an important celebration in Mexico and many Latin countries. On that page we also hid a woman selling a basket of chapulines (grasshoppers). People in Mexico snack on them! Would you like to try some?

MEXICAN CUISINE IS KNOWN FOR ITS BLENDING OF INDIGENOUS AND EUROPEAN CULTURES, AND CAN BE SPICY! POPULAR DISHES INCLUDE TACOS, ENCHILADAS, MOLE SAUCE, CHURROS, CINNAMON-FLAVORED HOT CHOCOLATE, AND AGUA FRESCA. DID YOU NOTICE ANY OF THESE IN THE BOOK?

Did you notice four animals hanging out at the pyramids? These animals are the symbols of the four tribes that lived in Teotihuacan: the jaguar, the coyote, the eagle, and the snake.

FRIDA LOVED AND OWNED ALL KINDS OF ANIMALS. WHAT ANIMALS CAN YOU SEE IN HER GARDEN? FRIDA'S BLUE HOUSE IN MEXICO CITY IS NOW A MUSEUM, YOU CAN VISIT IT – AND THE GARDEN REALLY IS MAGICAL!

Did you know there is real pink water on the east coast of Mexico? It's in lagoons called Las Coloradas. The water is pink because of the red algae, plankton, and brine shrimp that live in the salty water.

THE GIANT CRYSTAL MAZE WAS INSPIRED BY A REAL CRYSTAL CAVE CALLED CUEVA DE LOS CRISTALES, LOCATED IN THE STATE OF CHIHUAHUA. HUMANS CAN'T BE IN THE CAVE TOO LONG BECAUSE IT IS SO HOT AND HUMID. SOME OF THE CRYSTALS ARE AS LONG AS WHALES!

The place with the canals is called Xochimilco (hoh-chee-meel-koh), which means "the place where flowers grow." People rent boats and float all day, listening to music, buying food and drinks from small boats, and having lots of fun.

MEXICO
XOCHIMILCO

Mexico . . . did you know?

DIA DE LOS MUERTOS: Remember the people-flies? They were getting ready to celebrate Dia de los Muertos, or the Day of the Dead, celebrated at the beginning of November. Because the butterflies come back to Mexico at the same time of year, tradition says that the monarchs are dead souls returning to earth.

DESERT: Antonio's desert is called the Sonoran Desert, the hottest desert in Mexico. Some of the cacti grow up to 40 feet tall! It's common to eat prickly pear cactus. Want to try? Mexico is also the home of lush jungles and fir tree forests!

FEATHERS: Remember Lily's magic paintbrush? Ancient Mexican people believed feathers had special powers, and they were also used as money. The word for feather in Spanish is pluma.

FRIDA KHALO: Frida Kahlo was an important artist who lived in Mexico City from 1907–1954. Her enchanted blue house is called La Casa Azul. Frida had a hard time walking, so she laid in bed for many hours painting. Her imagination was wild and she had a big influence on Mexican culture.

MARIACHI MUSIC: People in Mexico love all kinds of music, and they love dancing too. Happy mariachi music often fills the air. There are usually guitars, violins, trumpets and a few singers in the band. Would you want to join a mariachi band?

PAPEL PICADO: This is a traditional folk art from Mexico that involves cutting out intricate patterns on colorful tissue paper. Papel picado is used to decorate for celebrations, or simply brighten up a place.

PINATAS: Piñatas are containers most often made of cardboard and paper which are filled for celebrations such as birthday parties. Blindfolded children take turns trying to break the piñata with a stick to release the treats that are inside. Have you ever tried to break a piñata at a party?

PYRAMIDS: The pyramids Lily and María visit are in Teotihuacan, (te-oh-tee-wah-kahn) which means "the place where gods were born." An old myth says that the gods chose this special place to create the center of the universe. Over 200,000 people lived in this city at one point!

QUETZALPAPALOTL: Remember the silly bird at the pyramids? His name means beautiful butterfly. There is a palace in the pyramids with the same name filled with pictures of quetzal birds and owls. It is thought that the rich people lived there when it was a big city. If you could have a palace, what would it look like?

RED MOUNTAIN: To solve the riddle, Lily and María have to find a red mountain, which is a volcano. Did you know there are lots of active volcanoes in Mexico? The most famous is nicknamed El Popo, short for Popocatépetl, which means smoking mountain in Aztec. El Popo has erupted over fifteen times!

SUN and MOON: In Nahua myths, the sun and moon were created where the pyramids sit. The Pyramid of the Sun is one of the biggest in the world, 210 feet tall! Lily climbed The Pyramid of the Moon, which looks out over the ancient city. There are secret tunnels and caves under the pyramids. Want to go explore?

SOMBRERO: Felipe's hat is called a sombrero, first worn by Mexican cowboys, called vaqueros. The wide brim protects the vaquero's face from the hot sun. Now, sombreros are often worn by mariachi bands.

THE MAGICAL
Monarch Butterfly
MIGRATION

SNIFF, SNIFF! Monarchs have incredible smelling abilities: the sensors on their antennae are 5,000 times more sensitive than human noses.

WHAT'S IN A NAME?
María and her family are monarch butterflies, or "mariposa monarca" in Spanish. The Mazahua tribe calls these butterflies "daughters of the sun," and the Purépecha people call the monarchs the harvester butterfly, because they appear when it's time to harvest the corn.

WINGS AND THINGS. The male monarch butterfly has a black spot on each hind wing. The monarch female has noticeably thicker wing veins, which give her a darker appearance.

HOW LONG DO MONARCH BUTTERFLIES LIVE?
Although our story is about generations of María's family, most monarchs do not live more than a few weeks. This makes the migration even more amazing, because the butterflies return to the same forests without ever being there before.

FRIDA LOVED BUTTERFLIES. We think Frida and
María would have been amigos, because Frida had a picture of butterflies hanging above her bed.

PUPA

CATERPILLAR

EGG/LARVA

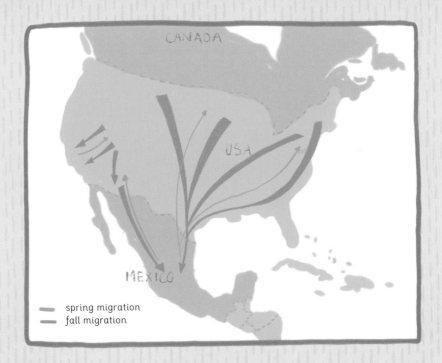

spring migration
fall migration

A LONG WAY TO FLY! Each October, the monarchs fly up to 3,000 miles to get to Mexico from Canada, the longest route of any insect! These clever creatures use an internal compass to figure out where to go and fly up to 100 miles a day.

MARIPOSA MOUNTAIN. Millions of butterflies fly to the same forests in Mexico every year for the winter. They huddle together on fir trees at night and if you listen closely, their wings sound like rain falling. Once the sun comes out, the sky is filled with orange wings – it is magical! Many of these places are now reserves to protect the monarch butterflies from deforestation.

RIDDLE DIDDLE. Remember the yellow flowers from the riddle? Those are called chichupa blossoms, and there are lots in the forests in Mexico where the butterflies live. Monarch butterflies also love butterfly bushes, verbena, zinnia and of course milkweed. Milkweed is very important because it is the only plant monarch caterpillars will eat. María's necklace is made of a milkweed flower!

BUTTERFLY

Hi friends,

That was one razzly-dazzly adventure in Mexico! Can you believe I painted my very own wings? Where do you think I should go next? Australia? Italy? Every little corner of this big, beautiful world?

Please send me all your ideas and stories. And draw pictures! I love getting mail. I wait for the snail every day to see if I have letters.

Lily Huckleberry
This Little Street
PO Box 7630
Berkeley, CA 94707

Or email me on the computer!
Lilyhuckleberry@thislittlestreet.com

Easy-peasy! Make sure to write your address, so I can send you a surprise from the Worldwide Adventure Society!

I love making new friends. I can't wait to get your notes!

Adventures Await!
Love,

Lily

A note from the authors

Thanks for coming along on this adventure! As we were writing,
we traveled to Mexico to research its fascinating culture.
(Little did we know that we wouldn't be using our passports for awhile!)
We explored the pyramids and found ourselves in a cave, digging
for treasure. From the mariachi band that came on board
our boat in Xochimilco, to Frida's magical blue house, Mexico charmed
its way into our hearts again and again.

On our last day, we hiked into the monarch forest, not sure it was
going to be warm enough for the butterflies to leave their cozy trees,
but then the sun came out and we were immersed in butterflies.
It was an experience that was so much better than our dreams.

Many thanks to everyone who helped us along the way, especially
the beautiful people of Mexico who taught us so much –
your warm welcome made us feel right at home.

To all of our readers, we hope this story helps your ideas come alive.
We didn't know where Lily would take us when we took this leap,
but we are so glad we did.

Jackie + Audrey

AUDREY SMIT is the founder of This Little Street, a design company with a colorful and happy aesthetic. Audrey created This Little Street to be driven by meaningful stories to build a colorful world where kids can dream, discover, and learn. Originally from France, Audrey lives in Berkeley, California with her four silly, adventurous little girls, who give her a good run for her money and are constant sources of inspiration for her work.

FOLLOW HER ON INSTAGRAM @THISLITTLESTREET

JACKIE KNAPP has mentored and taught kids worldwide for the past two decades, most recently developing a creative arts program that empowers children to collaborate on original films. Jackie has degrees in counseling and psychology, and believes that the stories kids read shape the adults they become. This is her first children's series, inspired by a Thursday Adventure Club concocted for Audrey's girls and her own gypsy spirit.

FOLLOW HER ON INSTAGRAM @GYPSYJAC